The Little Purple Mardi Gras Bead

D1244146

Julie P. Rowley

Illustrated by John R. Paquette

PELICAN PUBLISHING
NEW ORLEANS

The word "Pelican" and the depiction of a pelican are trademarks of Arcadia Publishing Company Inc. and are registered in the U.S. Patent and Trademark Office.

Library of Congress Cataloging-in-Publication Data

Names: Rowley, Julie P., author. | Paquette, John R.
Title: The little purple Mardi Gras bead / by Julie P. Rowley ; illustrated
   by John R. Paquette.
Description: New Orleans : Pelican Publishing, 2017. | Summary: "Ready to
   ride in his first Mardi Gras parade, a small, plain purple bead learns
   about Carnival and is excited to be caught by a paradegoer who will value
   him"— Provided by publisher.
Identifiers: LCCN 2016053643| ISBN 9781455623440 (pbk. : alk. paper) | ISBN
   9781455623457 (e-book)
Subjects: | CYAC: Mardi Gras—Fiction. | Parades—Fiction. | New Orleans
   (La.)—Fiction.
Classification: LCC PZ7.1.R79 Li 2017 | DDC [E]—dc23 LC record available at https://
lccn.loc.gov/2016053643

Printed in Korea
Published by Pelican Publishing
New Orleans, LA
www.pelicanpub.com

To my daughter Rebecca, who sparked my imagination and creativity, as well as to my grandchildren, Abigail, Alice, and Jacob, who continue to be my inspiration

Special thanks to my sister Lisa for her encouragement and support, and to my dad, John R. Paquette, for making my story come to life with his colorful illustrations

Once upon a time, in the city of New Orleans, a little purple bead on a tiny necklace was about to ride on a float in a Mardi Gras parade for the first time. The little purple bead was very excited as he watched all the beads being unpacked and placed on the float. He was also afraid, because he had no idea what would happen next.

"Excuse me," the little purple bead said as loud as he could to the other beads. "Can anyone tell me what happens during a Mardi Gras parade?"

The largest bead on a beautiful strand of polished pearls cleared her throat and said with a soft Southern accent, "Mardi Gras means 'Fat Tuesday' in French. It is time to celebrate before Lent begins. There is always a king and a queen of the parade."

"Is there a princess too?" asked the little purple bead.

Laissez Les Bons Temps Rouler

Let the Good Times Roll!

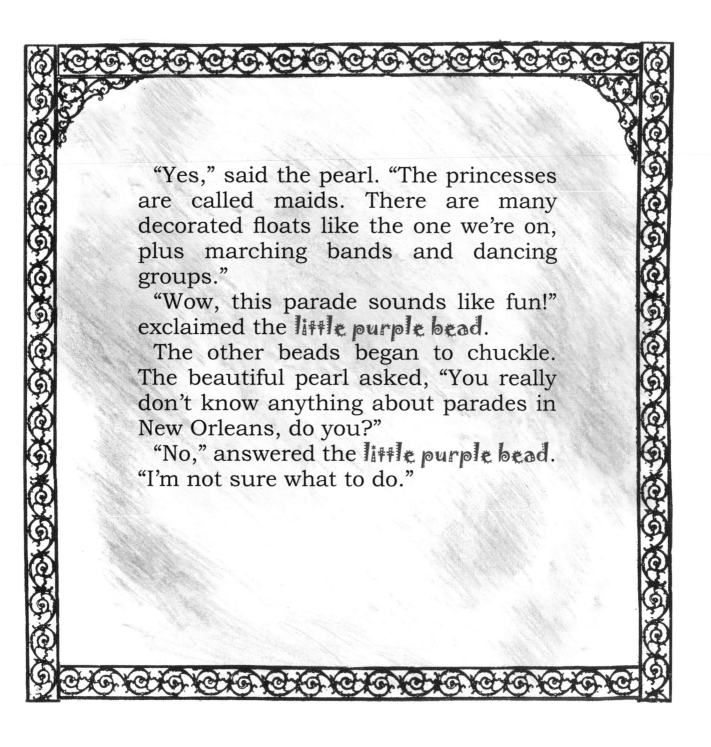

"Yes," said the pearl. "The princesses are called maids. There are many decorated floats like the one we're on, plus marching bands and dancing groups."

"Wow, this parade sounds like fun!" exclaimed the little purple bead.

The other beads began to chuckle. The beautiful pearl asked, "You really don't know anything about parades in New Orleans, do you?"

"No," answered the little purple bead. "I'm not sure what to do."

The beautiful pearl explained, "Each one of us will be taken off a hook and thrown into the crowd of people shouting, 'Throw me something, mister!' It is very exciting to be caught and worn."

Soon the floats started rolling. The parade had begun! The little purple bead peeked around the other beads to get a better view.

"Wow!" he thought to himself. "Those beads look like they're having so much fun!" He watched them being tossed high into the air and flying into the crowd's outstretched hands.

The little purple bead couldn't wait until he would have a turn too. Soon all the beads and trinkets were being thrown off the side of the float by the maskers.

Hanging next to the beautiful, polished pearl was another strand of beads that blinked purple, green, and gold—the colors of Mardi Gras. On this blinking necklace was a bully bead.

The bully bead looked down at the little purple bead and said in a loud, rough voice, "I don't think you need to worry about not knowing what to do. If you are thrown, I don't believe anyone would even try to catch you. You'll probably just fall to the ground and get stepped on. No one wants a plain, ordinary bead like you. Everyone out there wants fancy beads. All the cheering people try to catch us when we are thrown."

The little purple bead was no longer excited about being in a Mardi Gras parade. He wasn't even afraid anymore; he was only sad.

Meanwhile, toward the end of the parade route stood a beautiful little girl dressed as a princess. Everyone around her was having a great time listening to the music of the marching bands, watching the dancing girls, and catching the colorful beads and trinkets being thrown from the floats.

But the little princess hadn't caught any beads. She stood unhappily, watching as the floats passed. The people around the princess tried to share their beads and trinkets with her, but she didn't want any of them. She wanted to catch her own beads. Unfortunately, because the princess was very small, every time she would reach up to catch a pair of beads coming her way, many hands above her would snatch them up first.

"I would like to catch even just one pair of beads all by myself. I never catch anything," the beautiful princess cried.

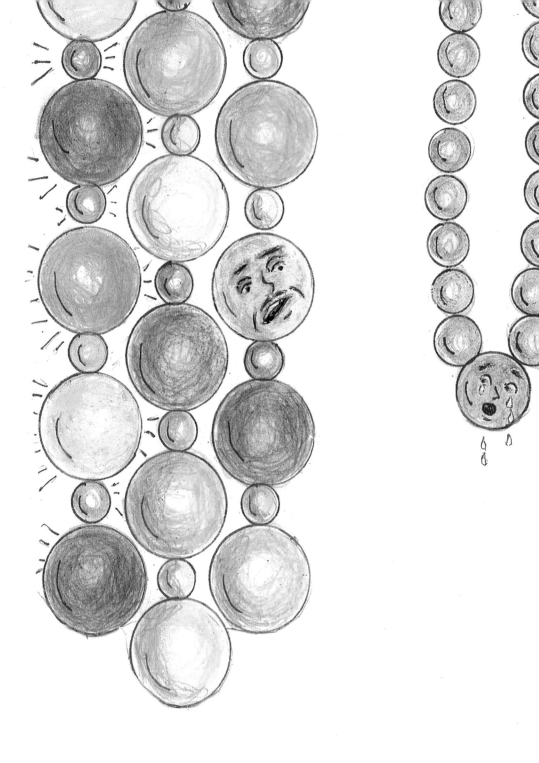

Back on the float, the little purple bead realized that the parade was about to end. Unless he was thrown very soon, he would never have a chance to fly in the air and be caught. As tears fell from his eyes, he spotted the little princess in the crowd. "Oh! How I would love to be caught by that beautiful princess," he wished.

The bully bead still hung on the float and exclaimed, "It's too late now, buddy! Looks like all of us left behind will have to wait until next year."

The little purple bead didn't want to give up, so he kept wishing and wishing that he would be caught by the beautiful princess.

The princess kept wishing too. Her mom whispered into her ear, "Stretch out your arms, jump up and down, and scream 'Throw me something, mister!'"

The beautiful princess did what her mom suggested. She held up her arms as high as she could and yelled at the top of her voice, "Throw me something, mister!" But the masked riders on the float didn't hear or see her. As the very last float was passing, the princess stood in silence, afraid that her wish would not come true.

All of a sudden, a rider snatched the little purple bead off his nail and threw him from the float. But was it too late?

The little purple bead flew through the air and spotted the princess among the crowd. He twisted, twirled, and wished as hard as he could to be caught by her. It was as if the princess's wish and the little purple bead's wish met and formed a breeze to carry him.

As the beautiful princess looked up, the little purple bead magically landed over her head and fell gently around her neck.

"Look, everyone," the princess shouted. "I caught my own beautiful beads! This is the prettiest little necklace that I've ever seen."

The little purple bead on the necklace was overjoyed, for he was now being worn by someone who loved him. It truly was a happy Mardi Gras.

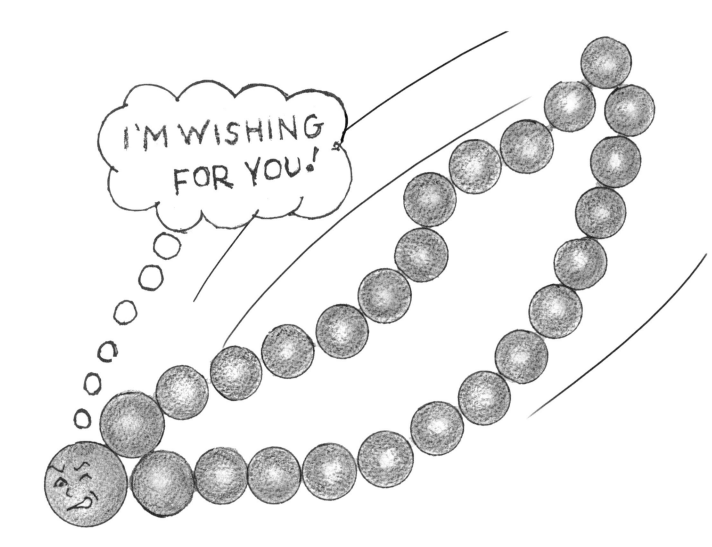

So whenever you catch a tiny strand of little purple beads, remember that it could be a wish coming true.

Author's Note

The **Little Purple Mardi Gras Bead** is a story created in anticipation of Mardi Gras Day. It was inspired by my young daughter Rebecca's imagination at bedtime. Mardi Gras is always an exciting, fun-filled day with family and friends. The food, music, colorful floats, and costumes are great; but as a young child, catching beads was perhaps the most special part of the day. It was a wish come true.